BRADFORD
IN PHOTOGRAPHS

DAVE ZDANOWICZ

AMBERLEY

First published 2021

Amberley Publishing
The Hill, Stroud
Gloucestershire, GL5 4EP

www.amberley-books.com

Copyright © Dave Zdanowicz, 2021

The right of Dave Zdanowicz to be identified as the Author of this work has been
asserted in accordance with the Copyrights, Designs and Patents Act 1988.

ISBN 978 1 3981 0303 0 (print)
ISBN 978 1 3981 0304 7 (ebook)

British Library Cataloguing in Publication Data.
A catalogue record for this book is available from the British Library.

Typesetting by SJmagic DESIGN SERVICES, India.
Printed in the UK.

FOREWORD BY VISITBRADFORD.COM

Dave Z, in his own distinctive style, captures the iconic landmarks and landscapes of Bradford, a book filled with stunning images, uncovering the beauty of Bradford. Every one of these places has its own interesting story to tell. We urge you to discover them all ... and we invite you to share our passion for the city.

visitbradford.com

ACKNOWLEDGEMENTS

Thank you to my amazing family (Mum and Dad, Treacy, Jack and Oscar) and friends for your help and support making this book. A special thank you to Visit Bradford for writing the foreword for the book. I really appreciate your kind words.

Thank you to Kenko Tokina, Hoya, Vanguard, Lume Cube, Pluto Trigger and TOG24.

I would also like to thank the following people and organisations: Intro 2020, Karen Shaw and Alex Cowland from *Northern Life* magazine, Emma Clayton and the Bradford *Telegraph & Argus*.

I would like to thank Bradford Council for supporting my work. Rizwana and Imran from Royds Hall Manor, Len Palmer and John Coulton at Bradford Council, Michael Shackleton and Bradford City FC, Su Holgate and Vicky Leith from Bradford Theatres, Natalie Everett and Bradford Museums, The National Trust and East Riddlesden Hall, Bradford Grammar School, Bradford Waterstones and The Midland Hotel

A huge thanks to my followers on Facebook, Twitter and Instagram. I really appreciate you all taking the time to view and share my photography.

ABOUT THE PHOTOGRAPHER

Born and raised in Bradford, West Yorkshire, Dave Zdanowicz is a landscape photographer who is very proud of his home city.

Dave has achieved a lot so far in his photography career. He has provided images for a number of books, as well as images to major TV networks including BBC, ITV and Sky, and his pictures have regularly been published nationally and internationally in newspapers and magazines.

Website: www.davezphotography.com
Facebook: www.facebook.com/davezphoto
Twitter: @davez_uk
Instagram: @davez_uk
Email: info@davezphotography.com

INTRODUCTION

It is a great honour to release *Bradford in Photographs*. The images in this book have been captured and selected from my vast adventures in and around the city over the last few years.

I was over the moon when Amberley suggested a photographic book on my home city of Bradford. I really wanted to show the city and the surrounding areas in a positive light and showcase some of the best locations. I hope it inspires people to visit the area and local residents to explore some of our wonderful landmarks.

In the course of taking these photographs I have explored moors and hills, reservoirs and parks, and cliffs and villages throughout the city. Each picture represents a unique moment, captured at a particular time of the year.

It has been a pleasure revisiting some of my favourite destinations around the city as well as discovering new places for the first time. Whatever the weather, whatever the time of year, Bradford is a fantastic place to explore.

I hope you enjoy the book.

Dave Zdanowicz

Dobson Locks

Baildon Moor

Harold Park

Leeming

Goit Stock Falls

Cow and Calf Rocks, Ilkley

Haworth Main Street

A view from Clayton

City Park

Roberts Park

The Broadway

Alhambra Theatre

Bingley mist

Baby of the North statue

Leeds & Liverpool Canal, Apperley Bridge

Bolling Hall Museum

Bowling Park

The Foundation Stones

Bridge Street

Town Hall clock

City Hall clock at night

Bradford at night

Bradford Cathedral

Bradford City Football Club

Bradford City Hall

Bradford City Hall

Bradford City Hall

City Park reflections

Bradford Grammar School

Bradford Grammar School's Main Hall

The Boathouse Inn, Saltaire

Peel Park

Peel Park

Cartwright Hall

Chellow Dene Reservoir

Chellow Dene Reservoir

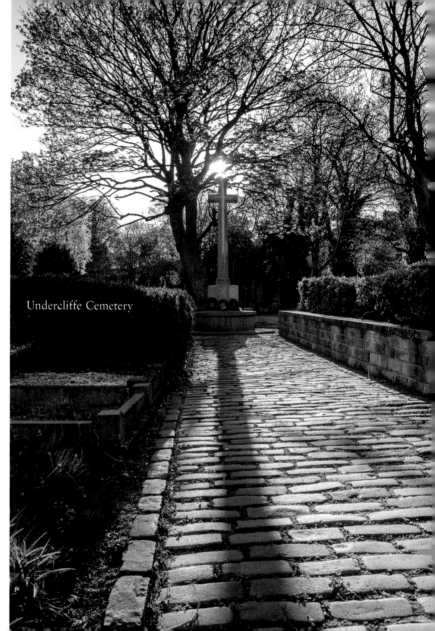

Undercliffe Cemetery

Bridge Street

Norfolk Gardens

Brow Lane, Clayton

Cleckheaton tree

Cemetery Road

Wyke

Cow and Calf Rocks

Denholme

Jug Dam, Low Moor

Esholt

Waterstones,
Wool Exchange

St Blaise Square

Woodside

Harden Beck

Bronte Parsonage, Haworth

Thornhill Bridge

Haworth train station

Heaton Woods

Horton Park

Harold Park

Wool Exchange

Hustlergate

Bradford Industrial Museum

Ivegate Boar

SUNBRIDGEWELLS

Welcome to the
World of Pure Imagination

BARS

Heaton Woods

Saltaire United
Reformed Church

Waterfall, Judy Woods

Judy Bridge

Judy Woods

Albion Street

Lady Hill Park

St David's Folly, Harden

Chapel House

Lister Park

Norman arch at Lister Park

Little Germany

Chapel Street, Little Germany

Little Germany

Ivegate

Lower Laithe Reservoir

Middleton Woods, Ilkley

Midland Hotel – old railway platform

Midland Hotel

Midland Hotel

Near Station Road, Wyke

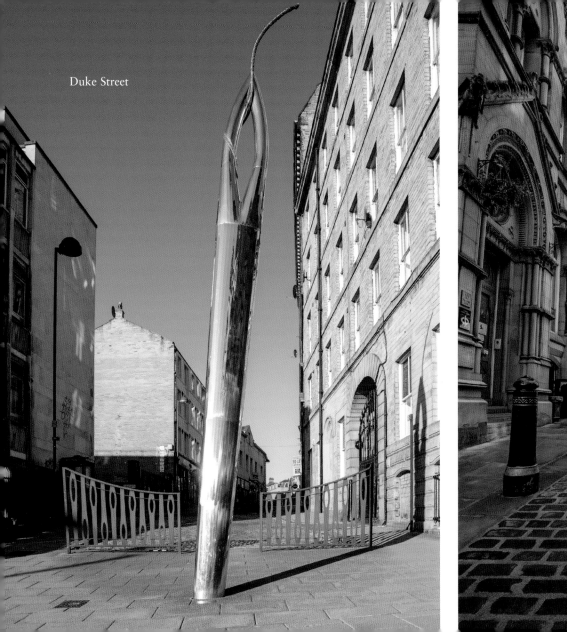

Duke Street

Piece Hall Yard

Oxenhope sheep

Paper Hall

Haworth in the Snow

Peel Park

Yorkshire Penny Bank

Queen Victoria memorial

Queensbury

Red Beck

Richard Dunn Sports Centre

Saltaire United
Reformed Church

Henry Street, Saltaire

Saltaire

National Science and Media Museum

Junction Bridge, Shipley

Barkerend Road

Shipley Glen Tramway

The Old Glen House

Shipley

St George's Hall

St George's Hall

St Ives Estate, Bingley

Sunbridge Wells

The Broadway entrance outside

Thornton viaduct

Northcliffe Park

Northcliffe Woods

Goit Stock Waterfall

Wibsey Park

Bolling Hall garden

Saltaire – New Mill

Clayton

Manningham Library

The Marlboro, Carlise Road

City Park

Royds Hall Manor

St James' Church, Baildon

Leeds & Liverpool Canal

Five Rise Locks, Bingley

Bingley Town Hall

Cliffe Castle Museum

Horton Country Park

Tyrrel Street

Long Bridge,
Haworth

Silsden

Beckfoot Bridge

Grand Mosque

Haworth Moor

Godwin Street

Shipley Glen

City Hall

Cartwright Hall, Lister Park

Telegraph and Argus Building